Mosaics for the Home and Garden

Creative Guide, Original Projects and instructions

Sigalit Eshet

Copyright © Sigalit Eshet
All rights reserved.
First Print Edition: 2016

www.sigalitart.net

sigalit@sigalitart.net

No part of this book, text, photographs or illustrations may be reproduced or transmitted in any form or by any means whether electronic, optical or mechanical (including photocopy, recording, Internet and e-mail). Commercial use of any kind of the content of this book is strictly prohibited without an authorization detailed in writing by the author.

Readers are permitted to reproduce any of the items/patterns in this book for their personal use. Any use of the items/patterns for commercial purpose is not permitted without a prior permission of the Author.

Thank you for respecting the hard work of this author.

Disclaimer

All do-it-yourself activities involve risk, and your safety is your own responsibility, including proper use of equipment and safety gear, and determining whether you have adequate skill and experience.

Some of the resources used for these projects are dangerous unless used properly and with adequate pre-cautions, including safety gear.

Some illustrative photos do not depict safety precautions or equipment, in order to show the project step more clearly.

Some projects are user-submitted, and appearance of a project in this format does not indicate it has been checked for safety or functionality. Use of the instructions and suggestions is at your own risk.

I disclaim all responsibility for any resulting damage, injury, or expense. It is your responsibility to make sure that your activities comply with all applicable laws.

Content:

Introduction	5
Mosaic tools	6
Adhesives	8
Grout	9
Grout making	10
Materials	12
What base should I use?	13
Working methods	14
Using the mosaic cutter	15
Mosaic process - step by step	16
Project: square tile terracotta pot	17
All about breaking plates	20
Project: Birds on a round pot	22
Project: Pitcher with polymer clay flowers	27
Pots with mosaic glass	30
More pots and pitchers	33
Metal tables	35
Mosaics on walls	37
Making stairs:	40
Summary	42

Introduction:

Welcome to the colorful stone path. I'm thrilled to use this space to share a little bit of the mosaic world with you. Here, I'll share my experience with examples, explanations and photos.

In this book you will find a few practice projects that show the process of creating the mosaic from start to finish, along with several photographs. Mosaic can be done on almost every surface. For the purposes of this book I have chosen to focus on mosaic projects for the home and garden—terracotta pots, tables and wall hangings.

If you want to decorate your garden with handmade crafts that will last for many years, mosaics are the way to go. In this book you will learn how to make every project a cheerful and bright addition to any home or garden.

The range of possibilities is endless with mosaics, and I want to open a window and show you many different options so that anyone will be able to choose the style that suits their home.

Even if you don't have any experience with mosaic work and the process seems complicated, I invite you to try. This book you will show you simple and clear explanations that will lead you step by step through creating your own mosaic work.

My name is Sigalit: I'm a mosaic artist, and have taught mosaics for several years. In this book you will find mosaics works made over the years by me and my students. The emphasis is on projects that fit into the garden, but of course they will fit into any home, big or small.

Now, we have a lot of work ahead of us! Happy reading and most importantly—have fun!

Mosaic tools

Basic mosaic tools are inexpensive and easily attainable (in the list below I also included some materials for advanced use):

Cutting tools:

Mosaic tile cutter – for cutting and grinding ceramic tiles. You can get these in hardware stores.

Wheeled glass nipper – for cutting glass and plates.

Ceramic cutting machine – for advanced cutters, used to cut ceramic into straight and accurate tiles.

Hammer – for cutting thick ceramic, or when you want to cut random shapes. Please note that when you cut ceramic with a hammer, you should wrap the ceramic with an old towel and place it on top of a thick wood or metal surface.

Mosaic tile cutter   **Wheeled glass nipper**

Safety equipment:

Safety Goggles – to protect your eyes from ceramic fragments. Use it when you cut the ceramic.

Dust mask – used this when making the grout.

Preparation tools

Pencil – for drawing the desired pattern on the substrate material.

Ruler – to mark straight lines.

Latex gloves – to protect your hands from scratches and dirt.

Rubber gloves – put these on before you start working with grout.

Carbon paper – to copy your design from paper onto your substrate material.

Plastic tools – for grout mixing, tile collecting and gluing.

Small brush – for cleaning the surface from dust and small particles.

Thin screwdriver – for cleaning tile adhesive residue.

Tweezers – for the placement of small parts.

Adhesives

For proper use of glue, always read the manufacturer's instructions. Use the glue that is most comfortable for you to work. It is very important to adjust the glue to the platform on which you are working. On wooden bases we use white glue—for indoor works only that will be away from water and direct sunlight. When we make a metal base mosaic we will use adhesive tile—this way the table can stand outside in all weather conditions with no problem.

PVA glue – for sticking ceramic tiles onto a wood surface.

Paintbrush – for adhesive application.

Mosaic tile adhesive – for sticking ceramic tiles onto metal, clay or ceramic pots

Glass glue – for sticking tiles onto a glass substrate (like E6000).

Wooden mixing sticks – for mixing grout and applying the tile adhesive.

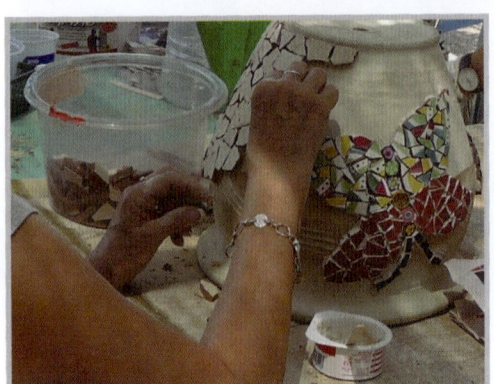

Grout

Grout – to fill the gaps between the tiles.

NOTE: There are different types of grout. Most of them come in powdered form, which you will need to mix with water according the manufacturer's instructions. Grout also comes in different colors, so choose the right color for your work. You can also mix acrylic paint into white grout to make your own custom colored grout, but if you do this, be sure that the final work is not exposed to the sun or water.

Working with the grout can be messy, so wear appropriate clothing and put on gloves before starting.

Water – for making grout and cleaning.

Small squeegee – for gripping and putting the grout on straight surfaces.

Sponge or cotton rags – for grout cleaning.

Old newspapers – to put under your work to maintain a clean work surface.

Grout making

Grout used to fill the gaps between tiles - usually walls and floor tiles. There are some artists that infect density and prefer not to use a grout.

In the mosaic work the grout used as finishing, filling the spaces between the cutting tiles. In addition it strengthens the work and unites all the parts to create a whole piece of work. The grout moderates the differences in height between the cut tiles and slides the mosaic work.

The grout is available in white or varied colored. White grout can blend with acrylic or color pigments, in case the work stays at home.

Choosing grout color: You can use an opposite color, to emphasis your work – in this case, a dark gray will be a great choice. You can use a color that blends with your design. In any case – don't try to fix the grout color when the work is done, even if you don't like it – just live with it!

Applying a grout - step by step:

1. Wear a dust mask to protect your face.

2. Put in plastic bowl grout in an appropriate quantity and color. In time, your experience will taught you about the appropriate amount. If there's not enough grout - Mix again grout + water in the same bowl.

3. Pour water in the grout bowl. Mix with a wooden stick until the texture is like a cream. Note the manufacturer's instructions.

4. Put on your rubber gloves.

5. Put old newspapers under your work.

6. If there are parts of the substrate you do not want to get dirty, they must be protected with painter's tape before grouting.

7. Apply the grout: on a flat surface, use a small squeegee and spread the grout on the surface until it fills in all slots and holes. On three-dimensional base spread the grout by hand and stuff it into the holes between the tiles.

8. After a few minutes when the grout starts to dry, start cleaning: wet the surface using a clean cotton rag or a sponge. Use a wet and dry rag several times until the work is clean.

9. IMPORTANT: Make sure to wet the work. Wetting the grout makes it harder and prevents cracks. Don't skip this step!

10. If revealed "holes" after cleaning, fill with grout, let it dry and clean until you get a smooth and clean work.

11. Adhesive residue can be cleaned with wooden skewer or a thin screwdriver.

12. At the end of the work you can be polish it with a wet wipe.

13. If some tile falls during grouting, clean the place well. Wait until the end of grouting process and then glue the fallen part (you can use a speed glue), wait for completely drying and fill the holes with grout.

Materials

Mosaic materials are varied and include:

Colorful ceramic tiles – in different shapes and sizes.

Glass tiles – these come in uniform size squares and in many colors. They have one smooth flat side (which should face up), and a rough side (faces down; this is the side to which glue is applied).

Stained glass – comes in many colors and textures.

Ceramic square tiles – available in many colors, textures and shapes; come mostly on a square mesh.

Ceramic or porcelain plates – using safety precautions, these can be broken or used to cut your own tiles from.

Broken cups – for more abstract, non-uniform pieces in your mosaic, you may wish to break your own glass.

Beads, seashells, glass beads, buttons, glass nuggets –use this to decorate and enrich your work.

Mirrors – breaking mirrors might be considered bad luck, but they add a beautiful reflective touch to any mosaic piece.

Polymer clay – use polymer clay like Fimo to create your own designs, or decorate your mosaic work.

What base should I use?

Mosaic tiles can stick to almost any surface: wood, metal, concrete, terracotta, glass or ceramic. (Note – it is not recommended to stick on plastic bases or tools).

If you want to put your work in the open air, outside, use a metal, concrete, glass or ceramic platform - not wood. Be mindful that wood-based mosaic projects should be displayed indoors only, as wood can warp and soften when exposed to the elements.

It is very important to adjust the glue to the platform on which you are working. On wooden bases we use white glue—for indoor works only that will be away from water and direct sunlight. When we make a metal base mosaic we will use adhesive tile—this way the project can stand outside in all weather conditions with no problem.

Check the strength of the substrate before starting your work. When working with ceramic tiles, the final work can be incredibly heavy.

A tapestry mesh is a base for mosaic that will be mounted on walls. This is the basis for works like wall tiles, stairs or large wall murals. We stick the mosaic on a mesh cut to the shape and size of the desired surface, and after it dries it is glued into place with mosaic tile adhesive.

In most of the works in this book I used tile adhesive – it is a strong adhesive and designed to withstand outside in any weather.

Working methods

After getting to know the working materials, we can begin selecting the working surface. If you want to put your work outside, you should start with a small terracotta pot.

Be sure to have the colorful ceramic that you want to work with prepared in advance.

For your safety, put on your eye goggles before cutting the ceramic to protect your eyes from small ceramic shards.

I recommend you to start with ceramic that is a little softer than others for your first mosaic piece, for easier cutting. After you've gotten comfortable, then you can start working with different tiles grades.

Using the mosaic cutter

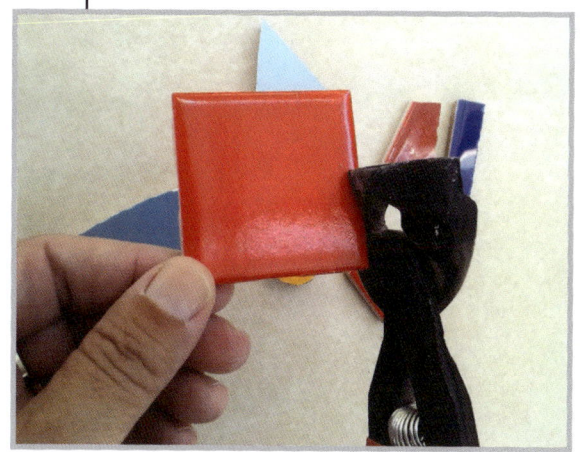

Hold the bottom of the cutter with your dominant hand, having the curved side facing towards the ceramics. Hold the ceramic tile in your non-dominant hand, and in the other one, hold the bottom of the cutter handle.

Hold the ceramic tile with the cutter in a straight or diagonal direction to suit the type of crop you want, and clip!

If you want to cut small pieces or to shape the tile, hold the tile by the widest part of the cutter and clip.

Mosaic process - step by step:

1. Choose a work surface you want to work with.

2. Select the design or the ceramic colors you want.

3. Collect the working materials: ceramics, glass, cups, plates, beads, shells or stones - whatever suits your design.

4. Plan the design and draw it in with a pencil. You can copy it with copy paper or freehand sketch.

5. Cut the materials according to the design you want. Choose the size and shape cutting - large or small parts, square or cut to freeform shapes.

6. Stick with the appropriate adhesive. If there are elements in the design like figure or a flower, begin with them and then stick the background.

7. Let the glue to dry at least for 24 hours.

8. Apply your grout using manufacturer's instructions.

9. Clean and dry the project with wet and dry rags.

10. You're done! It's time to pride with your new creation

Project: square tile terracotta pot

Mosaic terracotta pots are ideal for home and garden decoration. They act as a nice focal point of color, and come in many shapes and sizes.

You can use pot coated with different materials. This one is made with square tiles in different colors, which you can get in ceramic stores. There's no need to cut anything, as this is quite simple mosaic work. You can create it in your own color tiles scale.

You will need:

Ceramic or terracotta pot

Colored square tiles: Black, white, dark blue, mid sky blue, red and orange, 1-2 cm.

Tile adhesive

Wooden stick

Thin screwdriver

Blue grout

Grout Equipment: mixing bowl, water, a wooden stick, rags, gloves, Small squeegee and dust mask

Old newspapers

1 Take a terracotta pot; a round one is recommended for this project.

2 Prepare and collect the tiles.

3 With tile adhesive, start sticking the tiles, row after row: with a wooden stick, put a small amount of adhesive tile on the back side of each tile and stick it into place. The first row is a colorful one, so use a mix colors of the tiles you choose. With a screwdriver, take out the spare adhesive from the tiles.

4 The second row is made up of small light blue tiles – 1 cm squares, then blue tiles.

5 Now stick 2 rows of black and white tiles, alternating colors.

6 Next 2 rows – light blue mixed with orange, red and blue. Finish the rows with one more round of small light blue tiles and black.

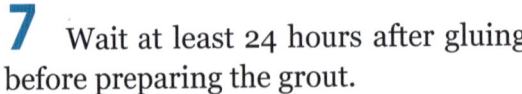

7 Wait at least 24 hours after gluing before preparing the grout.

8 Prepare the grout in your desired color (a gray-blue in this case). Cover the working surface with an old newspaper. Put gloves on, mix your powdered grout with water in a plastic bowl to the manufacturer's instructions and spread over the pot with your hands until it's completely covered. Let it sit for about 10 minutes.

9 After a few minutes when the grout starts to dry, start the cleaning process: use a wet rag or sponge to clean the grout from the tiles. Alternate using a wet and dry rag several times until the pot is clean. **IMPORTANT**: Make sure to wet the pot. Wetting the grout makes it harder and prevents cracks. Don't skip this step!

10 That's it! The pot is finished! You can clean it with a wet wipe to give it a shiny finish.

All about breaking plates

You may think that breaking plates is very simple: just throw it on the floor, and there are a lot of pieces of broken plate to collect... right? But if you want to control the size, shape and design of the broken glass, use a wheeled glass nipper and follow these instructions:

Breaking plate – taking out the frame design

1 Hold the plate in one hand and the nipper in the other one. Keep it straight.

2 Click! The plate breaks easily.

3 Hold on to one half of the plate and keep cutting in the same way.

4 After you finish cutting, when you have a lot of broken plate pieces, (like cake slivers), it's time for separating the design from the plate. Hold the piece of plate in your hand, in the other hand hold the nipper – close and straight to the edge of the plate with the design, and click.

5 Keep cutting each piece with the nipper until you get the right size and clean design.

6 If you want to use smaller parts in your work, just keep cutting each piece to undefined shapes with the tile nipper until you get the size you want.

7 IMPORTANT: For your safety, wear goggles when cutting plates to protect your eyes from small pieces of sharp ceramic.

Breaking plates – taking out the center

Sometimes we find a plate with a nice drawing in the center of the plate. To use it as a part of the mosaic work, use the following steps:

1 Hold the plate in one hand and the nipper in the other one, diagonally.

2 Click. Notice you cut parts you don't need, away from the center image.

3 Continue cutting this way around the plate.

4 The first round is complete. Now it's time for fine-tuning! Gently cut the sharp edges away with the nipper.

5 That's it – the plate is ready to use! It can be use as a table center, picture to hang, or in any mosaic work you choose.

Project: Birds on a round pot

You can stick almost any material you want on clay pots – ceramic tiles, beads, glass, broken cups and plates, and much more—just use your Imagination!

For this terracotta pot I used mostly broken ceramics. You can adjust colors as desired or according to the materials you have.

You will need:

Round terracotta pot

Colored ceramic tiles – orange, blue, and white

Broken cups and plates – blue colors, brown, and flowered

Tile adhesive

Wooden stick

Mosaic tile cutter

Wheeled glass nipper

Pencil

Thin screwdriver

Brown grout

Grout equipment: mixing bowl, water, a wooden stick, rags, gloves, small squeegee and dust mask.

Safety goggles

Old newspapers

1 Copy the birds to the pot. Use 3 or more, according to the pot's size.

2 Start with the bird's head: First cut an orange triangle for the beak. Then, use something round for the bird's eye: a bead, a round ceramic shape or, in this case, a flowered round piece of polymer clay. Cut the blue ceramic into small parts and fill in the head. Spread tile adhesive on the back of each piece of tile and stick it to the pot at the right place.

3 The bird wing is made from small pieces of a broken plate (see the instructions above).

4 The bird's body is made from another broken plate. Finish sticking all the bird's parts to the pot and add 2 small orange ceramic rectangles for the legs.

5 Do the 2 other birds in the same fashion as the first one. You can switch the color of the tiles between the wing and the body; the birds do not have to look exactly the same.

6 Now, let's add some ground: draw a curved line under the birds. A brown plate or cup will fit for this part. If you don't have one, use brown ceramic tile.

7 Add some flowers: cut from plates with the tile nipper, as close as you can to the flower to get smaller part. Stick it between the birds.

8 Fill the background with white ceramic – cut to small pieces.

9 Wait at least 24 hours after gluing to grout. Use brown grout for this pot to emphasize the colors. See grout instructions.

10 That's it—in just a few steps you have a beautiful scene for your garden pot.

Project: Pitcher with polymer clay flowers

Some pitchers are used for decoration, and can be a gorgeous addition to any home or patio. They have a special charm that makes them more impressive than the typical store-bought flowerpot.

This special vase combines ceramics and millefiori flowers made from polymer clay. You can also use beads or cut your own colorful ceramic tiles.

You will need:

Round terracotta vase

Ceramic tiles — blue, white, orange, red, and black

Millefiori polymer clay flowers — sliced and baked into rolls

Tile adhesive

Wooden stick

Mosaic tile cutter

Pencil

Thin screwdriver

Beige grout

Grout equipment: mixing bowl, water, a wooden stick, rags, gloves, small squeegee and dust mask.

1 Choose a tall pitcher. Cut flower petals from white ceramic, 5 petals for each flower, 4 flowers total.

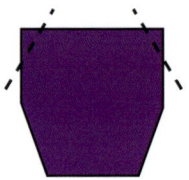 

2 Making the petals: cut a rectangular shape, crop the bottom edges and round the top with small cuts. Stick a round bead, glass nugget or polymer clay circle at the flower center with tile adhesive. Stick 5 petals around the center of each flower.

3 Take several beads or Millefiori Fimo circles and fill the gap between the flowers. You can also do it with small cuts from colorful ceramic.

4 Cut the blue ceramic into small pieces, with a tile cutter or hammer for rougher patterns. Stick the ceramic to the pitcher with tile adhesive. Let the glue dry for at least 24 hours before moving on to the next step.

5 Grout – it is better to use a white or beige grout color when using colorful beads of polymer clay. See the grout instructions at the beginning of this book for more details.

6 Once you've grouted, grab your rag and give your pitcher a good cleaning!

Pots with mosaic glass

You can also use glass in your mosaic work. The glass adds shine and bright color. It is important to be careful when working with glass and to cut it while wearing gloves to avoid injury.

You can use broken dishes, colored glass pieces you have collected, or leftover glass from other projects. Cut the glass with your wheeled glass nipper, making random or straight shapes.

For glass tiles on terracotta pots, use regular tile adhesive. You can combine it with ceramic tiles or stick only glass to your mosaic work.

Terracotta pot, colored glass parts; beige grout

A decorative pot, white ceramic, mirror elements, and colorful glass

Terracotta pot, colored glass parts, mirrored elements, broken plates; blue grout

A pitcher, mirror elements, and colorful glass; black grout.

A small pot, yellow ceramic, mirrored elements, and colorful glass

Small pot, light blue glass squares, glass pieces: white, green and blue; blue grout

More pots and pitchers

colorful pot made of ceramic, broken cups and plates

A big pot, colorful ceramics, yellow and red glass squares

A very big pot made of ceramic, glass, mirrored elements, broken cups and a center broken plate

Pitcher made of orange and black ceramic tiles, broken plates

Large pot with birds created from ceramic, plates and cups

Metal tables

A mosaic table is very practical - beautiful and unique from one side, on the other hand is easy to clean. Such a table can be made in any size, shape or color. You can make it with ceramic mosaic tiles or glass.

Mosaic tables can stand indoors or outdoors. They are strong and durable. You can order such a table with a metal frame that makes a nice finish or a flat plate – in this case pay attention to the edges; they must be straight and smooth.

The working method is like any other flat base: after choosing the design, draw it on the metal table substrate. If your base is dark, use white pencil.

Choose the ceramic and other materials for your mosaic table. If you want to use the table, notice that all the ceramic you choose should be about the same height in order to get a smooth table surface. If it's for decoration, then you can combine and mix other kinds of materials without kipping a flat surface.

Here are some samples of metal tables:

Small decorating table, no frame. Color combination: brown, yellow, white. Ceramic tiles and glass nuggets. At the center: painted tile.

Square metal table, framed. Colorful ceramic, black lines

Small coffee table, no frame. Ceramic tiles; flowers, background cut in big and small pieces.

Mosaics on walls

If you have a stone fence, stairs, exterior wall or window frame made of concrete - you can decorate them with colorful mosaic. There is no need to panic - the work is done on the desk at home, and only after you finish will you stick the mesh to the wall.

You will need:

Tapestry mesh

Nylon – for putting behind the mesh or plastic bag

Colored ceramic tiles

Masking tape

PVA adhesive and paintbrush

Tile adhesive

Mosaic tile cutter

Pencil

Grout

Grout equipment

Safety goggles

1 Prepare your design – draw or print it on paper, actual size.

2 Stick the paper to the table with masking tape. Cover it with nylon or a plastic bag (this will prevent the mesh from sticking to the paper).

3 Cut a tapestry mesh slightly larger than the design and tape it to the nylon.

4 Collect the working materials: ceramic, glass, small tiles, cups, plates, beads, shells or stones - whatever suits your design.

5 Cut the materials according to the design you want. Choose the size and shape of the cuttings - large or small parts, square or cut into free shapes.

6 Stick the pieces to the mesh with PVA adhesive.

7 Let the glue dry for at least 2 hours.

8 Gently peel the mosaic mesh from the nylon. Cut the mesh as close to the design as you can.

9 Apply a tile adhesive to the wall and put the mesh on it. Press the tiles to the wall gently.

10 Clean up the excess adhesive if there is any and allow it to dry for 12 hours (don't do this on a rainy day).

11 Apply grout (on the wall).

12 Clean and dry using a combination of wet and dry rags.

Making stairs:

Mosaics on stairs are very beautiful, especially if you have gray concrete stairs. There are lot of options and designs that you can do – a design that starts on the bottom step and ends at the top stair, combinations of colors, the same design on all stairs, etc. The technique is the same as shown before – on mesh.

I recommend doing a mosaic on the front part of each stair, not on the part that people walk on. This way it is possible to combine many materials and get a unique result that will last.

1 Measure each stair separately. There might be slight differences between them.

2 Prepare a paper in the right size.

3 Follow the mesh instructions – design, collect materials, stick them to the mesh and allow it time to dry.

4 Spread adhesive tile on the proper place on the stairs.

5 Stick the mosaic-mesh to the adhesive and push each tile into place. If the strips are too long, you can cut them before gluing them to the stairs.

6 Clean the leftover adhesive and let it dry for at least 24 hours.

7 Grout – on the stairs.

8 Clean and enjoy!

Summary

Thank you for the time that you have taken to read this book. I truly love the art of mosaic and feel the need to share the knowledge I have gained over the years, as it is a great privilege for me.

The variety of options you have when creating a mosaic project is endless! If you want to decorate your home and garden, mosaics works are a beautiful and unique fit. Beginners can start with square flowerpots, as we have learned in the book, in different colors—each one according to his or her own taste. Those who love to cut their own tiles can combine broken cups and plates with glass or other hardy materials. It's a beautiful addition to any home or garden, and can be a nice family activity.

We have seen various examples of mosaic pots - with figures and drawings, colored glass, flowers and many other examples. Use your imagination to create a mosaic pot that is perfect for your home or garden!

If you have a balcony, or if you are hosting guests in your garden, mosaic tables are very suitable for this purpose. Remember to use the ceramics of the same height as you prepare the mosaic table.

Even your walls and stairs can be decorated - we learned the technique of using tile tapestry mesh. You can start with small projects with simple designs like flowers or animals, then work your way up to planning a mosaic for the wall or stairs.

I was happy to introduce you to the mosaic world. My garden is full of mosaic pots. Even if you do not have a garden, I'm sure you'll find a place for a mosaic pot you made yourself. It's not complicated—sometimes it takes time, but the result is worth the effort!

Starting today, collect your broken plates, cracked glasses, or even old beaded jewelry—the more colorful the better. Why throw away items with such wonderful artistic potential? Let's reinvent them and turn them into a wonderful mosaic creation!

More books from this author on Amazon:

 **Mosaic Hamsas**

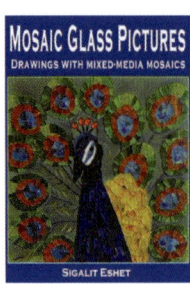 **Mosaic Glass Pictures**

 **Mosaics: Great Ideas and Projects**

 **The Magic Mesh - Mosaic Mesh Projects**

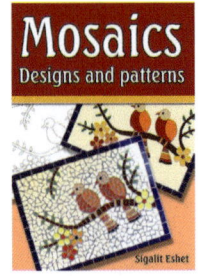 **Mosaics - Designs and patterns**

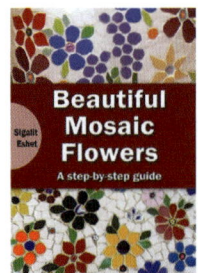 **Beautiful Mosaic Flowers**

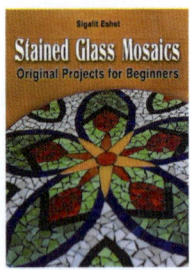 **Stained Glass Mosaic**

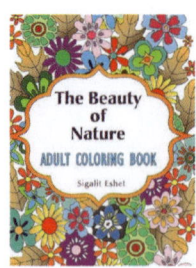 **The beauty of nature: Adult coloring book**

Printed in Great Britain
by Amazon